FREIGHT BROKER WITH CARE

Guide on How to Start and Grow Your Freight Brokerage Business Like a Pro

I0472021

TOSH COLE

TABLE OF CONTENT

INTRODUCTION V

Why Are Freight Brokers In Demand In Today's Economy.......... x

CHAPTER ONE
What You Need To Know As A New Freight Broker 1

CHAPTER TWO
Startup Freight Broker Software Programs 13

CHAPTER THREE
Need To Know Accessorial Codes...25

CHAPTER FOUR
How To Earn Big As A New Freight Broker 33

CHAPTER FIVE
How To Cold Call.. 39

CHAPTER SIX
Cold Call Script 45

CHAPTER SEVEN
How To Negotiate Rates..57

CHAPTER EIGHT
How To Dispatch... 67

CHAPTER NINE
How To Handle Claims As A Freight Broker 85

CHAPTER TEN
A Typical Day As A Freight Broker..91

CHAPTER ELEVEN
Tips Towards Becoming A Successful Freight Broker............... 97

CONCLUSION 103

INTRODUCTION

This introduction to freight brokering serves as an informative guide to what you will need to know to become a freight broker. If you are afraid of the phone or do not like to talk on a phone, then this business is NOT for you. A freight broker will spend 90% of his/her time on the phone. Cold-calling customers, talking to customers, talking with carriers, etc.

With that said, let's move on to the important things that you will need to know, with the most important factor being Customer Service. It does not matter if you are a broker or an agent working for a broker, if you do not take care of your customers, you won't need to worry about finding carriers. And if you do not take care of your carriers, you won't need customers. Thus: no customers, no carriers, no business—get the idea?

If you want to open a freight brokerage, there are several things you will need to do. First step is to get your authority. Next is your bond, your BOC3, your insurance, and your UCR (enforcement for the UCR begins 01/01/2009). Then you will need the proper training in order to open and effectively operate your brokerage. And if you desire to be an agent, get the proper training as well. You will need to know the same things the freight brokerage knows. After all, you will most likely be working under a brokerage. Below are some of the basic but important things you will need to know to become a freight broker or a freight broker agent:

The Industry

Freight brokers arrange for the transportation of cargo between shippers and motor carriers. Nearly everything you touch throughout a given day has been transported by a motor carrier. The industry is enormous. Most cargo is shipped with either a dry van, a refrigerated unit (reefer) or a flat bed. This occurs both within local markets as well as long distance and coast to coast.

Freight brokers, then, seek, identify and get set-up with shippers, manufacturers, growers and distributors who have cargo to transport and who rely upon freight brokers to provide trucks.

Motor carriers may be either large trucking companies who hire their own employee drivers or carriers who are independent drivers (Owner Operators).

Freight brokers earn commissions for their matchmaking skills. They are also known as "truck" brokers, "transportation" brokers and "property" brokers. And the brokerage industry can span not only trucks but air, rail and ocean liners.

Brokers are governed by the Federal Motor Carrier Safety Administration (FMCSA) of the Department of Transportation (DOT). There is no governing body other than these. There are no tests or exams given to pre-qualify freight brokers.

What shippers are looking for:

Usually, shippers work within cost constraints. So the rates for carrier services often depend on how much these shippers will pay. Though, supply and demand may sometimes determine the rate for particular loads. In all, shippers are looking for carriers who will move their cargo safely, efficiently and cost-effectively. And they are looking for brokers who conduct business honestly, reliably and with an excellent service-oriented mentality.

What carriers are looking for:

Carriers are looking for good rates. They also work within cost constraints. If motor carriers are knowledgeable about what their operating costs are, it helps them remain competitive. Knowing what is needed to maintain equipment, pay personnel and make a profit. This can make the difference of making it or breaking it.

Consequently, a freight broker is required to use good negotiating skills to complete a "competitive" transaction whereby everyone is satisfied—shipper, carrier and broker.

What brokers are looking for:

Brokers may first locate shippers who have cargo to ship and then look to motor carriers to "cover" the load. Or brokers may have motor carriers on hand who are seeking cargo to haul. In either case, the broker wants to make a match or cover the load.

New brokers will spend many hours on the phone searching for both shippers and carriers. With experience, however, brokers learn to work proactively where both shippers and motor carriers initiate much of the business.

This of course all depends on how well the broker performs. Getting both shippers and carriers to rely upon them is one of the primary objectives of the broker. This is when business starts to mushroom.

When brokers get set up with shippers, it is important for the broker to do a credit check in order to avoid getting stuck with a poor-paying shipper.

And before brokers work with carriers, the broker needs to ascertain how qualified carriers are. A carrier may be ready, willing and able to complete a haul; but the broker needs to document the carrier's status—legal, insurance and operational.

The business concept, then, is simple enough – a freight broker finds shippers with cargo, then finds carriers to transport the cargo and then makes a commission for hooking them up.

Freight broker opportunities offer a work-from-home benefit, low startup requirements, minor overhead expenses, and minimal formal educational requirements. And the tools of the trade consist of a computer, fax machine, telephone, and file cabinet.

WHY ARE FREIGHT BROKERS IN DEMAND IN TODAY'S ECONOMY?

There are several reasons why freight brokers are in demand in today's economy. Some people aspire to do freight brokering services, that's why they need to understand how the industry works before gambling away themselves into the business. To start this kind of business, you will need a potential data as a source of information on how to handle competition in this industry, from the existing brokerage firms to other brokers that are more experienced than you.

Today, businesses keep on growing at a fast rate. And it is getting increasingly harder to catch up with the groove of the businesses that require freight services. There will be an increase of demand with cargo loads if the customers also increase their need to travel their merchandise to several regions or ports. When the customer increases their demand, the company will be put into pressure to increase their cargo load in delivering their merchandise, products or goods. The shopping establishments are the most common customers of some companies that really need freight services.

A business makes their product to other businesses that run on selling the products. Bigger companies need to distribute their finished products from one place to another. If these companies do not possess the ability to transport their own products, they may need someone to transport their merchandise to another place or they may need a freight service. This is a great opportunity for freight brokers to take an action of doing business with these companies by offering them proposals and making a guarantee to provide good service for and with them.

As long as there's a steady incline in the increase of the demands made by consumers, companies will be put into pressure to keep the supply line going, of which transporting their goods will be a major part of the logistics involved. And, unlike the normal phase, transport might not be enough. As long as there is business between the producer or maker of the product and the company who sells the product, the logistics is always there. Brokers, on the other hand, will not be waiting for the clients to come to them, they will be looking for more clients every now and then. And clients as well will also be looking for competent brokers that can meet their needs and wants.

IMPORTANCE OF FREIGHT BROKERS IN TRUCKING INDUSTRY!

Freight in general terms refers to goods that need to be transported from the place of production to where it can be utilized as a commodity. For freight shipment, various modes of transport can be availed depending on the requirements. Airlines, ships, and trucks are the three main modes that are used globally for shipping of goods. These days, intermodal freight transport has gained its importance when the cargo safety is of utmost importance. Freight brokers help to create new owner operator jobs when any such requirements arise.

Now the BIG question is: how will the manufacturers or producer companies avail a efficient freight transport system to distribute their goods safely and on time? And there goes the role played by freight brokers. The freight broker acts as a link between the companies or individuals that need shipping service and the truckers and owner operators that provide shipping service. The shipment price is decided keeping in mind the rate which is beneficial to all the three parties involved for the goods shipped. By paying a little commission to the broker the shipper can get the required reliable shipping service without putting in efforts to find one themselves. Some companies hire a competent broker to take care of the complete shipment procedures of their goods.

Freight brokers help in preventing the services of efficient load boards in which they track all the trucking industry information and updates from the load boards. They would actually come to know of any available loads or if any company is in need of the broker service. Simple bidding by a few clicks of your mouse button and the job will be yours. The broker, in turn, will contact the shipper and the trucker to accomplish the task. This is both economical and reliable for both parties. With the professional service by the broker, the shipper can track the real time location of the shipped goods; whereas the trucking companies and individual trucker can get the quick payments for the goods delivered by the freight brokers in between. This ensures that the process of the delivery goes smoothly.

HOW TO CHOOSE A FREIGHT BROKER

A freight broker's job is all about logistics. The broker liaises between manufacturers, wholesalers and distributors to ensure safe and punctual transportation of goods to the designated destination point of resale. Profit on the transactions is known as freight brokerage.

As a profession, it has its origins at the early part of the last century. Licensed brokers are either companies or individuals, and the companies which contract them may rely wholly on them for their shipping needs, thus doing away with the need for a department of their own. There are currently about four thousand licensed freight brokers in the U.S., although only about half work as such full-time. Formal qualifications are not a legal necessity, although there are institutions offering training in the specialty and issuing diplomas. Licenses are issued by Federal Motor Carrier Safety Administration (FMCSA) and they must prove adequate insurance coverage to cover client losses in order to be able to operate.

When choosing a freight broker, bear this point in mind and check carefully because to hire a motor carrier authority is not always the same thing. Multiple transportation modes are a must. There should be alternatives available if anything goes wrong during the operation. How does the broker choose its carriers? Their selection criteria are very important. Not all carriers are equally trustworthy or reliable. The lines of communications are vital in this industry. Ask brokers how they match loads to carriers, how they confirm a correct pick-up and even view a selection of correspondence.

Information on freight companies is freely available on website directories, such as American Freight Companies at FreightCenter.com. This useful resource lists freight companies according to the following categories:

Freight Companies, Common Carriers, Shipping Companies, Trucking Companies, Motor Freight, Freight Services, Truck Load Freight, Furniture Shipping, Rail Freight and Special Freight Services. All the listed freight carriers have negotiated some kind of discount with American Freight Companies. How long has the company been operating? The first couple of years of any new business are fraught with problems and cash flow difficulties. As such, any established company has proven its worth. If you do not know much about a freight broker, use this as your basic criterion.

FREIGHT BROKERS & BROKER AGENTS

What's the difference between a freight broker and a broker agent? And which way is best to follow?

These are common questions from those interested in this industry. Let's try to shed some light on these questions.

1. A freight broker (also called a truck broker) is fully self-employed and is required to obtain his or her authority. He or she will do his or her own invoicing to customers and will pay the motor carriers. Essentially, the truck broker is running a complete business.

2. A broker agent works for another freight broker and does not need to obtain a broker authority. The agent works under the authority of his or her broker and is not responsible for invoicing or paying the trucks.

Pros And Cons To Each Option.

❖ First, a fully self-employed broker is required to get his or her authority but he or she retains 100% of the profit on each load. Further, the freight broker is totally responsible for invoicing the customer and making collections as well as paying the motor carriers. Having sufficient capital and good cash management skills are an absolute necessity. Since time is required to run an entire business, the broker has relatively less time to search for new customers and find trucks.

❖ Second, a broker agent is not required to get his or her broker authority and, therefore, this option is less costly. But the broker agent splits his or her commission on each load with whomever they work under. Most of the agent's time is spent searching for new customers and finding trucks.

❖ Third, most brokers are seeking experienced agents. There are a few who will accept new inexperienced agents but these freight brokers are far and few in between. If an agent is new or inexperienced, the broker normally does not want to spend a lot of time training or "hand-holding".

To recap, as a broker agent, you don't need your broker authority. You work under the authority of another truck broker. It's possible to begin as either a freight broker or broker agent and then switch to the other. The two fundamental differences are the scope of the duties and responsibilities and the fact that the broker agent does not need their authority.

Regardless of whether you work as a freight broker or broker agent, you may work out of your home. And you will meet and work with customers and carriers over the entire country.

Startup equipment

The following are the tools you require when starting as a freight broker:

- A good computer with a high-speed internet connection,

- Preferably two telephone lines (one could be either a cell phone or internet telephone),

- A good fax machine,

- Proper education and the drive and determination to succeed.

For both brokers and agents, good, comprehensive training or on-the-job experience is absolutely essential.

Here are a few topics you can expect to learn when you take freight broker or broker agent training:

- ✓ How to use the load boards
- ✓ How to find shippers
- ✓ How to search for trucks
- ✓ How to talk to shippers and dispatchers
- ✓ How to pre-qualify your motor carrier
- ✓ How to calculate rates
- ✓ Step-by-step procedures for booking a load
- ✓ How to get set-up with your motor carriers
- ✓ How to monitor and track your loads
- ✓ How to set-up and manage your information flow

Top Ten Lessons for Freight Brokers

As in every other part of the world, technology in the shipping world is exploding. Technology can be your best friend. Use it wisely.

1. Many freight brokers are moving to a more advance, streamlined, online freight quote system. This saves time and money. While they still have that personal relationship with customer support, this help them to get your shipments processed and out the door quickly.

2. A good freight forwarder, and a good freight broker will have an advanced technology system available for you. As one example, the benefits of a 3PL is that it has a web based log in portal that gives access to hundreds of carriers, instant data reports, EchoTrak that allows you to watch all shipments at your fingertips, and direct access to a team dedicated to finding the most effective shipping solutions.

3. A broker who more specifically does exported shipping, handles international customs papers, provides inland tracking services, warehousing, preparation of shipping, export documents and focuses on international shipments is called a freight forwarder. A freight forwarder is often called a Customs House Broker. These brokers can also provide customs clearance, consolidation, storage and insurance. All freight forwarders and brokers focus specifically on their shipping.

4. Brokers are middle men who negotiate shipments between the shipper and carrier. Essentially, these brokers have relationships with airlines, shipping companies etc. and use those relationships to get pricing for individual shippers. They are considered as intermediaries, liaisons or consolidators that bring many small shipments together in order to get discounted shipping prices. The services they provide are unique to their roles, as such, they do not offer any assistance outside of their tasks.

5. Avoid using the most generic national company. Your best bet for freight brokers is to run a local search online. Local companies will have the best pricing for your area, and the best relationships with local carriers too. For example, if I lived in Hawaii (I wish), I would search "Hawaii freight brokers". This will bring up a good list of the top 20 in the area to pick from. Use your networks, if you are part of a

chamber of commerce, or any networking group. Ask around, someone will have a good trusted referral for you. Good word of mouth is the best advertising.

6. Examine several qualifications like longevity, licensing, professionalism, testimonials, reviews and personal relationships. A good freight broker is someone you can call on the phone and get a quick response. There is nothing worse than feeling like your product is in the middle of Africa and you can't talk to someone to find out exactly where it is. This is especially important with a freight forwarder and international shipments. Be sure you have a person to talk to if you are shipping overseas, most especially if it's an expensive product. When it comes to a freight broker, it is good to make sure you choose a company that is not going to send you to a call center when something goes wrong. You need that personal service and customer care.

7. All brokers will have different pricing depending on their experience and the strength of their relationships with the carriers. Look for relationships with good strong reputable carriers. Also look for the quantity of carriers. If a broker only has a few carrier relationships, they do not have the depth to truly negotiate good rates. This is why looking for longevity is good too. Usually, the longer they have been a broker, the more competitive their rates.

8. All freight brokers should have a license from the Federal Motor Carrier Safety Commission (FMCSA). The best time to use a freight broker is always. They will always get you better pricing than your in-house shipping manager on the phone can get unless your shipping manager used to be a broker, and most brokers will back up their shipments to provide good customer care. A broker does not want to

lose your business, so, they will fight for you to make sure everything is running well.

9. It is important to check if they have insurance. Some brokers feel that it is not their responsibility. This is why you want personal contact with your broker. Make sure it is a large enough company to have insurance. According to their licensing, brokers should have insurance to help cover costs, but many do not. Also, if you are shipping very valuable items, ask about surety bonds. All large companies will have surety bonds, this is additional insurance that helps cover expensive damages and ensures that the company is held to high standards. A good broker will only work with transportation companies that meet this standard of quality of service that qualifies for insurance.

10. Be careful to know what your actual freight costs are. For example, you are sending a pallet from California to Canada. They quote you $78 for the 50 lb pallet. Awesome, you are thinking it is going to cost $78. Then when you get your invoice, you were charged: $20 for the liftgate to load the pallet on the airplane, another $20 for the liftgate to unload the pallet, another $35 for customs papers, $30 for broker fee, and then $25 for handling. Make sure that you know what price you are getting up front. A good broker will give you an all-inclusive pricing with no extra fees and charges except for duties and taxes. No one can fully predict duties and taxes when shipping internationally. An occasional unforeseen add-on is acceptable and usually happens, but be careful it is not 3 additional charges every shipment. If you are using an online freight quote system, make sure all charges are itemized before you book your shipment.

CHAPTER ONE

WHAT YOU NEED TO KNOW AS A NEW FREIGHT BROKER

Freight brokers search for shippers who need to transport their cargo from point A to point B. The broker then searches for a truck to move the cargo. The freight broker, then, puts the two together and acts as a middle-man, collecting a commission for his or her match-making skills.

There are a multitude of details and procedures that freight brokers follow. These procedures and details involve a great deal of coordination with both the shipper and the carrier.

Tips on Freight Brokering

Here are tips that will help a freight broker manage and coordinate their freight broker duties.

1) **Understand the needs and desires of both shippers and motor carriers:**

One of the biggest items of importance for shippers is "cost". Big companies employ entire departments of logistics to find the most cost-effective route and method to move their cargo. Some large shippers use their own trucks; some use freight brokers; and some allow their customer to arrange for the transportation. Smaller shippers rely more upon freight brokers to move their cargo. But both large and small shippers have "cost" at the top, or close to the top, of their priorities.

Carriers also place a priority on "cost". The current situation with high fuel costs and other high operating expenses have taken a toll on the availability of trucks. This availability, commonly known as "capacity", has been dwindling for several years. While shipper rates have increased, it's unlikely that rates have kept pace with a trucker's ongoing costs. The bottom line is, the broker needs to cover not only the actual costs but he or she needs to generate a profit on top of the costs.

2) **Understand that the freight broker must negotiate a win-win situation:**

Whereby everyone achieves their goals—shipper, carrier and freight broker.

Negotiating skills come easy for some people; others hate the idea of "haggling" with opposing parties. A good negotiator will understand that there is, at times, a "give-and-take". Knowing when to "hold 'em" and when to "fold 'em" can result in huge profits over time. The best way to exercise this "hold 'em and fold 'em" tactic will come from a broker monitoring his or her profit margin along with other important items such as volume of loads and days-in-collection on the receivables from shippers.

3) Pay attention to sound business fundamentals.

There are many successful freight brokers. Some have been around for quite awhile; others are just getting a good start. Of these successful brokers, each and every one, most likely, has relied upon sound business fundamentals. In fact, that's probably the very reason for their success. It takes more than just "brokering" to be successful. It takes a person to pay attention to marketing, cash management, planning and creating an operating blueprint.

Each of these four topics has had volumes written about them. Without attention to these, an freight broker is most likely doomed to failure – regardless of his or her brokering knowledge.

4) On finding shippers, find a strategy that works and then stick with it.

One of the biggest fears for beginning freight brokers is how and where to find shippers. It's not as difficult to find shippers as one might think. However, it is difficult to find good paying shippers who also have loads that are relatively easy to cover.

One of the most effective (but not easy) methods is to search the internet using unique keywords. There are plenty of various shipper directories available, but then you've got thousands of other brokers calling the same shippers as you are.

Unique keyword searches will likely uncover shippers who aren't being called by every freight broker in the country.

5) **When a shipper wants a quote or your rates, find out more about what you can expect.**

Some shippers will require quotes before they accept your set-up package. Some of their requests will involve 10, 15, 20 or more loads. Others will want a quote on just a specific load.

Sometimes the shipper is using you to gather information on how to price the load. Other times the shipper will throw your quote into a large pool of other quotes—and there it stays with the shipper having no intention of actually giving you the load.

Here's what to do: ask the shipper how often a particular load or loads are available. Daily, weekly, monthly? Make sure you understand if the shipper needs a dry van, reefer, flatbed or whatever. Refer to various pricing sources that provide the "going rates" for various lanes. If the shipper responds after you have given a quote that the quote is too high, tell the shipper that you'd like to try to cover the load for what he or she wants to pay. And ask for the order.

6) Get set up with as many carriers as you can regardless of whether or not you have a load for them.

There may be many, many incoming phone calls in response to some loads you have posted on the internet. Many of these calls will be "dead end" calls as the carrier is likely looking for a higher rate.

However, while talking to the carrier, get him or her talking about what THEY are looking for in regards to what lanes they

like, how many and what kinds of trucks they have, etc. If you "hit it off" with them, ask them if you can get set-up with them. Most likely they'll say yes. Then you have one more carrier in your database.

7) Be prepared for things to go awry at times.

In addition to "dotting your I's and crossing your T's, be not only mentally prepared for problems—have some specific plans in place.

For example, let's say you think you have a load covered. The carrier has said, "Yes, I want the load". And you've sent out your set-up package, you've received the broker-carrier agreement back. Next, you prepare and fax out the carrier confirmation. However, it doesn't come back and your phone calls go unanswered. So, what do you do? You first consider yourself "dropped".

However, you will probably be getting phone calls after you think you have a load covered. So what do you tell them? You tell them that you "think" you already have the load covered but you ask them to leave their name and call-back number just in case the load you just booked falls off.

These tips don't even scratch the surface when it comes to all the details and procedures that freight brokers face. They are, however, some of the more important items facing new and experienced brokers.

What experience do I need to become a freight broker?

The answer you'll hear most is "...be a truck dispatcher for a couple years, then look into becoming a freight broker." Normally, you'll hear this answer from freight brokers more than anyone else.

Before and after I became a broker, passing on the advice of becoming a dispatcher first, I often wondered what the logic was behind becoming a dispatcher first. Was this a required point of entry to the profession? Obviously not since I became a broker. Could it be that I would learn how to broker freight by being a dispatcher? No, I would learn how to dispatch trucks and deal with truck drivers. Then what could it be? Why was I being told to become a dispatcher first.

To answer the question: What experience do I need to become a freight broker? None. If you have any type of transportation experience, it is helpful and puts you ahead of the curve. Being a freight broker is more than just knowing the difference between a flat bed and a dry van. It's sales, marketing, computer skills, budgeting, people management, prospecting, presentations and much more altogether. All from the comfort of your office, be it at home or someplace else.

When I began my career as a freight broker, there weren't any schools or workshops one could attend. Even though I had an extensive career in the transportation industry, I didn't know much about the broker side. I started with only information about the trucking side, and it was an uphill struggle for the first 6 months.

Today, there are crash course schools you can attend for several thousands of dollars to online study sites that you can visit in a lesser amount. The choice is yours on which best suites your needs. I highly recommend that you invest in yourself by choosing a training method that will help you get around that 6-month curve at a price you can afford. By investing in yourself you will not only increase your chances at being successful, but you will also afford yourself the opportunity of becoming more profitable much quicker.

How to Select a High Quality Freight Broker

There are several reasons to use a freight broker, perhaps you have purchased an item across the country or need to get an item(s) shipped to your customer and you're looking for an easy, cost-effective way to get it done. Whatever the reason may be, this guide has been put together to help you select a high-quality freight brokerage company.

The below statements contains various items to look for including legal, insurance, quality and experience when selecting a freight broker.

LEGAL

> ➤ **Do they have a freight broker bond and operating authorities?**

As of October 1st, 2013, freight brokers are required by the FMCSA (Federal Motor Carrier Safety Administration) to have

in place either a BMC-84 or BMC-85 freight broker bond in the amount of 75,000 U.S. Dollars in order to maintain an active operating authority. The BMC-84 is a surety bond provided by an insurance company who is willing to guarantee the 75K in case the broker defaults on payments. The insured (broker) will pay a yearly premium of $1,000 to $12,000 in order to get this insurance in place. The BMC-85 removes the insurance company and is put in place by the broker themselves or a bank by putting $75,000 into a trust fund. The main benefit to a trucking company is that they have a bit more of a guarantee that they will get paid and that a less reputable broker isn't going to take the money from the customer and run without paying the trucker. The benefit to the shipper is very similar in the idea that they don't have to fear that after they pay the broker, the trucking company is going to come after them later if the broker takes off. This has helped reduce the amount of fraud in the industry as the broker now has to be financially stable before they even start. This is all fine if your in the USA or using a U.S. based broker but if you're in Canada it's a little different story. Currently the only province in Canada that regulates freight brokers is Quebec, who requires brokers to be registered with the CTQ. However in order to get active authorities the FMCSA stated that Canadian brokers need to obtain the bond as well. This has left many brokers in a grey area as the U.S. says they need it while Canada says they do not. Even if a Canadian broker wanted to get a bond it is very tough to find a U.S. or Canadian insurance company to quote it or offer it for a decent price. In conclusion, it is a good idea for all brokers to have it as it is beneficial to everyone and chances are if a Canadian broker has obtained a bond this might make them financially stable.

INSURANCE

> ➤ **Do they have proper insurance to protect your goods for transport?**

Chances are that the trucking company which the freight broker or freight brokerage company hires for you will have more than enough insurance to cover the value of your goods in the case of an accident, but it is a good idea for the broker to have insurance as well. You will want your broker to obtain proper insurance just in case the trucking company is running with expired insurance or the broker forgets to check the trucking companies insurance in the first place. Either way you want to make sure you are covered. A reputable freight broker will have this insurance in place and will likely provide a copy of it before you have a chance to ask for it. You will want to see a minimum of 1 million liability, 250k cargo (unless the value of your goods is higher of course). Also, having an error and omissions policy is always a good idea.

REFERENCES

> ➤ **Can you find non-bias references or referrals?**

A good freight broker will likely have reviews on Google about past shipments, however, keep in mind that these may be higher on the negative side as a person who had a good experience is much less likely to take the time out of their schedule to write a review in the first place. The best place to start would be from a friend or colleague who is in the shipping business. Chances are they have used one or more freight brokers before, and they should be able to point you in the right direction. The broker may also be able to provide references but unless it's from a big reputable company, it is likely not very useful.

EXPERIENCE

> **Has the freight broker ever done this before?**

Another important part to look for is if the broker has any experience brokering freight. You will want to make sure they know what they are doing, as moving freight isn't as simple as calling a trucking company and sitting back. They may have experience in moving dry van freight but no experience moving Agricultural equipment. Different types of freight have a lot of different requirements to get them shipped. If the item is crossing internationally, you will want to make sure the broker has experience doing that as mistakes may end up costing thousands of dollars. A experienced broker will be able to answer pretty well any question you may have about moving freight.

These are just a few of the key areas to look at before choosing a freight broker to move your freight. A broker that scores well in the above 4 areas will ensure your shipment is moved fast, on time and on budget.

CHAPTER TWO

STARTUP FREIGHT BROKER SOFTWARE PROGRAMS

Freight brokerage software provides you with dispatch tools to handle your order entry, links, load boards, posting, and searches. With such easy to use tools, you can process your order entries at faster speeds. All you need to do is show your data for prior shipments that you have entered for your customers.

Freight brokerage software enables you to have control over your selected shippers, products, and consignees that relate to your customers. You can use specially designed tools to control your dispatch section by highlighting the links for displaying your shipment counters.

The process enables you to reveal your work needed to the truckers so they can take care of the shipping right away. You have options for customer quotes, as well as dispatching. Shipments can now be assigned to your designated carrier and you can send customer orders and pickup requests straight to the trucker from the internet. When you have such tools, it makes it easier to organize your business.

The Features of Good Trucking Software

- **The software should be equipped with a dispatch program.**

This would keep track of all your operators and lets you know about the status of your orders.

- **The log program also makes freight broker software reliable.**

This keeps track on the number of hours each vehicle needs to cover and the cost that would be involved. This obviously helps you monitor the costs and assists you to get a better idea about your profit margin.

- **A fuel tax log program is another very important feature.**

Such a program would keep an account of the fuel tax of the different points in the journey of the vehicle. This would require that it keeps track of the different kinds of taxation rates. With this information, it would help you record the cost that it takes your vehicle to make the trip.

- **An accounting program in the software helps as well to keep you updated about each of the customer accounts.**

Some of the most popular freight broker software-programs are posted on the Internet. However, there are many types of software's available for truckers, some of which enable you to compare each trucker's software on the Internet.

The freight broker software and programs allow you to produce quotes, systematize, make bookings, invoice, and handle every single load effectively. This means you don't have to purchase other updates or install other software programs. Brokers design the truckers' software so you know that you are getting quality programs that produce expert results.

Some of the free load board programs provides you with the quickest and easiest method to locate loads and trucks. With this software, you have unlimited access to search trucks, loads and posts. You don't have to worry about installations instead, you subscribe to a website to receive the benefits of freight broker software.

With the latest trucker's software, you do not need a special computer. Instead, you can use any sort of computer that connects to the Internet via modem. The trucker software allows you to use Linux, Mac, or common operating software.

This gives you the ability to work anywhere there is an Internet connection.

FREIGHT PROGRAM SUBSCRIPTIONS AND FEES

On the Internet are programs that you can subscribe to. There are subscription software you can use anywhere. But there is a monthly or annual fee. You have a payment option. Several different packages are offered that give you choices to choose software programs that fit your budget.

The software isn't designed to locate shippers, but the vendors have a huge list of shippers on file in which you can gain access to by requesting the information. Not every company offers the same features in trucking software so it pays to compare the features and pricing for the freight broker software that interests you.

With the latest programs, truckers can now submit their quotes, books, invoices, and also organize their loads without having to install another software onto your computer. It is possible now to find trucks and loads with ease, which explains why so many truckers are searching for freight software designed by the experts.

Many of the programs available today come with tutorials, making it simpler for you to access the freight broker software with few hassles. Best of all, the programs are easy to use and you can connect online about anywhere in the world where Internet is available.

TOP 10 FREIGHT SOFTWARE PROGRAMS

1. ProTransport

Capabilities: Accounting, dispatch, safety compliance, maintenance, document management, two-way texting, IFTA reporting.

About the Company: With more than 13 years serving the trucking industry, ProTransport provides an all-in-one software solution for hundreds of carriers' businesses and administrative activities. ProTransport's various modules can be added and customized for fleets or freight brokerages of any size. The software integrates with various programs, including QuickBooks, GPS, fuel card providers, factoring companies, IFTA and more. ProTransport's simple dashboard and color-coded interface make the software's features accessible and easy to navigate.

2. Axon Trucking Software

Capabilities: Accounting, dispatch, maintenance, IFTA reporting.

About the Company: Axon has been a software provider for the trucking industry since 1982. The company claims the software's real-time integration with other programs enables clients to slash administrative time by 47%. Axon is also integrated with PC Miler truck routing, mileage and mapping software. There is also an App for this software for easy tracking.

3. TMW Systems

Capabilities: Dispatch, accounting, fleet maintenance, bid management, transportation management software.

About the Company: Founded in 1983, TMW Systems today has more than 2,000 customers ranging from small to large fleets. Customers can choose TMW's transportation management software or products specifically for dispatch, fleet maintenance or accounting. A subsidiary of Trimble Transport & Logistics, TMW claims to have a customer retention rate of more than 95%.

4. PCS Software

Capabilities: Dispatch, accounting, safety compliance, fleet maintenance, transportation management.

About the Company: For more than 20 years, PCS has provided transportation management software for both carriers and freight brokers across truckload, LTL and intermodal trucking. The company's mobile app and cloud-based hosting means the software can be accessed from any location at any time.

PCS Mobile Express provides two-way communication between drivers and dispatchers.

5. Prophesy

Capabilities: Accounting, dispatch, communication, load planning, safety compliance, IFTA reporting.

About the Company: A division of HighJump, Prophesy has 20-plus years of experience serving the trucking industry. Over the years, the company has expanded its suite of shipping, broker and trucking software for the Windows platform. Today, Prophesy claims that more than 12,000 trucking companies use Prophesy software products.

6. ITS Dispatch

Capabilities: Dispatch, accounting, IFTA reporting, fleet maintenance, load bidding.

About the Company: ITS Dispatch is the web-based software affiliate of the popular load board TruckStop.com. Like most other trucking software products, ITS Dispatch links with QuickBooks Pro and QuickBooks online. Customers can add software modules like file storage, IFTA reporting and other features as their trucking business grows. ITS Dispatch claims it has more than 50,000 registered users.

The Truckstop Mobile app includes features that allow drivers and dispatchers to communicate and share load documents.

7. Tailwind Transportation Software

Capabilities: Accounting, dispatch, safety compliance, quoting and orders, IFTA reporting.

About the Company: Tailwind has web-based software products aimed at trucking fleets, freight brokers, or brokerages that run their own trucks. Customers can choose among three software tiers—Standard, Pro and Enterprise—depending on the size and complexity of your business. Founded 16 years ago, Tailwind launched its first software-as-a-service application in 2015.

There App Launched in 2017, Tailwind POD Complete allows two-way communication with drivers and captures electronic proofs of delivery for orders.

8. McLeod Software

Capabilities: Accounting, dispatch, freight management, bid procurement, document management, customer relationship management.

About the Company: McLeod offers a variety of software products for more than 850 customers in the transportation industry. The company's flagship products are its LoadMaster dispatch software and PowerBroker for freight brokerages. McLeod also has software solutions that help customers manage paperwork, direct sales and marketing, and measure fleet performance.

The McLeod Anywhere application allows clients to track orders and fleet performance from their phones or tablets.

9. Trinium Technologies

Capabilities: Accounting, dispatch, fleet management, safety compliance.

About the Company: Trinium began as a software provider for petroleum distributors, but has now introduced a cloud-based enterprise software for intermodal trucking and container drayage companies.

10. TruckingOffice

Capabilities: Accounting, dispatch, maintenance, document management, IFTA reporting.

About the Company: TruckingOffice was developed by a fleet owner to help keep his company's invoicing and records organized. Today, the online software helps small trucking companies handle dispatching, accounting, IFTA reporting and maintenance schedules. There are two tiers of TruckingOffice software available—Basic and Pro—and carriers are billed by the size of their fleets.

BENEFITS OF FREIGHT BROKER SOFTWARE EXPLAINED IN DETAIL

Today's Freight Broker Software has innovative features and tools that make them worthwhile. Some of the cutting-edge programs have integrated features such as transportation management systems. The systems are designed to provide freight brokers with more profit from the efficient use of the tools.

- Now you can use programs to manage all your transportation and shipping activities combined from one location. You have easy tools to use for dispatching, routing, operations, tracing, carrier selection, and accounting.

- All of your accounting needs are covered since you have billing and collection tools to help you get the job done right. The Freight Broker Software allows you to focus on your work by providing you with TMS or transportation management tools and features from one system.

- These systems enable you to take care of non-asset based freight brokers and have integrated support for various shipping options including LTL or Less-than-truckload, TL or truckload, expediting, rail, etc.

- Today's broker programs speed up efficiency since the programs are web-based and comprise of freight management applications. You have continuing updates for your program that provides you with easy access to new features. Now you can maintain your programs with ease as well, since the software today is technology driven and have effective management systems.

- Using freight broker programs today allow you to calculate success while focusing on a single shipment. You have support and help to handle all your daily duties. All you need to use is the user-friendly dispatch tools, carrier rate selection, tracing and tracking, or the seamlessly integrated accounting tools.

- You also have detailed administrative reporting tools with sales staff portal and consumer access. There are some programs that organize data storage so that you know where your files are when you need them.

- With dispatching programs, you can reduce time needed to enter your orders and create your shipping documents. The web-based portals allow you to send order entries, reduce calls to your operation staff, since all your details are sent automatically.

- With carrier selection, you have shorter carrier research options so that you can improve your profit margins with ease. Now you can enhance sales with web-based sales staff portals. Freight brokers need all the help they can get when it comes to handling trucking tasks.

- With tracking and quality assurance, the brokers can automatically setup an advantage for tracking while reducing the amount of calls coming in for each shipment. Communication can be improved when you have shipping data tools to help you stay in contact with your customers and staff.

Freight Broker Software today provides you with all the right tools and features needed to do business the right way.

CHAPTER THREE

NEED TO KNOW ACCESSORIAL CODES

If you are a new shipper in the LTL (Less-than-truckload) world, it may seem like a big task at times, without a starting or ending point. It may seem like an overwhelming amount of information that a shipper needs to know, ranging from learning the NMFC classes, to the specifics, like who is the best carrier to haul your freight, and what price will they charge. This is just a glimpse of the freight world. Seasoned shippers, who have been in the business for 20-plus years, often find themselves being introduced to things that they didn't know, or thought they knew, and were totally wrong about. The freight world is a dynamic, fast-moving industry that warrants attention to details by Logistic Departments. With this being said, one of the trickiest topics to grasp, especially when a company first starts shipping freight, is Accessorial Charges.

Things That Can Cause Accessorial Charges

Most accessorial charges are tied to services at the origin or destination as part of your final bill, so it's best to pay close attention to every detail so you can provide accurate information to the carrier. The following examples are some of the most common accessorial charges.

1. **Ground Pickup or Delivery**

When a shipment arrives at an location without a loading dock, a liftgate or other means of transferring the freight from the trailer to the ground is required. Liftgate equipment isn't common on standard 28- or 53-foot trailers, so be sure you know the specifics of your destination's loading area and communicate that back to the carrier.

2. **Over-Dimensional Goods**

It's crucial for a carrier to know upfront if the freight they're transporting exceeds the size or weight limit of a standard shipment. Without reporting over-dimensional measurements, the carrier will have to adjust appropriately on-site and you'll likely face an additional fee.

3. Limited Access Pickup Or Delivery

A carrier may levy this fee if they're picking up or delivering to a location with limited access such as schools, military bases, prisons or construction sites. Delivering to these locations could be more challenging because they may not have loading docks, or they may require security inspections prior to entry.

4. Inside Delivery

Inside delivery or pickup is an fee for having a carrier deliver or pick up a shipment that goes beyond the tailgate of the trailer utilized. This service may be requested by either the shipper or the consignee and will be provided at an additional charge.

5. Change in Weight or Description Fee

If the correct weight or description is not specified on the bill of lading, the carrier may assess an additional fee for their correction.

6. Stop off

These charges typically occur when a shipment has two or more destinations. Multiple destinations require a driver to make several stops along the way, which could cause a delay for the other shipments they're carrying.

7. Residential Delivery

If a carrier has to travel into a residential area to deliver freight (whether it be a home address or a business), a residential delivery charge may apply. This is because of the complex nature and extra time needed to navigate a truck through a residential zone.

8. Lumper Service

A lumper fee is assessed when a third-party service is used to load or unload the contents of the trailer. The fee is common in the grocery distribution and the food warehousing industry.

9. Detention

If the carrier is delayed for any reason, detention charges may apply. Some detention time will be embedded into the shipping contract, but this charge typically begins when the driver is detained beyond the time noted.

10. Storage

If you need the carrier to hold your freight at their service center for a specific time period, you may incur extra charges. Additional expenses may apply because your goods are taking up space in their warehouse and equipment, which disables them from moving other shipments.

ACCESSORIAL CHARGES THAT MAY ACCRUE?

- **Shrink Wrap**

This is a fee which is chargeable when the shipper requires the driver to shrink wrap pallets.

- **Pallet Jack**

When a driver is required to load or unload a trailer with a pallet jack, a pallet jack fee may be tendered.

- **Layovers**

A layover fee may be charged to the shipper if they are the cause of the layover. If the layover was done by the carrier, then the carrier pays out-of-pocket.

- **Truck Ordered Not Used (TONU)**

Having a load fall through is inevitable. Most contracts will have a clause allowing for a TONU. There is only a charge if the truck is canceled after a pre-established cut-off time.

- **Deadhead**

This charge is the result of when shippers are charged the empty miles for preferred use of a carrier's equipment.

- **Tolls**

Modern toll collection methods have made travel on toll roads easier for vacationers. Carriers may charge shippers for tolls incurred during loaded miles.

- **Fuel Surcharge**

The fuel peg is the price on which contract pricing is based. Carriers may obtain fuel cost information from the Department of Energy's website. A surcharge is charged according to the current price of fuel. For instance, on the carrier's pricing table, the surcharge might be $0.05 if the current rate of fuel is between $3.509 and $3.559. This prevents the carrier from having to forecast fuel prices to stay in profit.

- **After-Hour Deliveries**

A carrier may charge a shipper for after hour deliveries if the carrier typically only delivers during business hours. This would not be a common accessorial fee for truckload carriers.

- **Border Crossing**

Similar to tolls, carriers may charge shippers any border crossing fees.

- **Cash-On-Delivery (COD) Fees**

Some carriers may be willing to receive COD payments at the time of delivery. In doing so, they might charge an additional fee to handle the money.

- **Non-Dock Deliveries**

This is not a common fee for truckload carriers, but it is a possible fee. If a driver has to deliver product other than to a dock, the carrier may charge additional fees to cover the labor.

- **Diversion Miles**

If upon arrival at a shipper or the end receiver, the carrier is told to drive to a different location, then divergent miles may be charged. There will typically be a ceiling mileage of which the carrier is willing to drive at no additional charge.

CHAPTER FOUR

HOW TO EARN BIG AS A NEW FREIGHT BROKER

Freight brokers inhabit a unique space in the overall transportation market. Brokers voluntarily insert themselves between shippers who want their freight delivered 100% on time, every time without a single error or loss, and trucking companies who most of the time do a good job, but who have to deal with the real world of stolen trailers, bad weather, road construction, flaky drivers and Acts of God. This is a recipe for "getting your blood racing".

1. **Use advertising and marketing techniques that work.**

Track your marketing efforts so you can concentrate on the techniques that work and eliminate the ones that don't.

Smyrna, Tennessee, freight broker Cathy Davis said small giveaway items, such as pens, note pads, caps and T-shirts, work well. Company newsletters with personal and industry information also get a good response. She said donations to fundraising events may be helpful (depending on the event and the degree to which it's promoted), but the impact of website sponsorships is questionable. She recommended developing a three-panel printed brochure that's easy to include with letters, invoices and checks.

Chuck Andrews, an Indianapolis-based freight broker, builds name recognition by placing periodic ads in association newsletters as well as in annual association and industry directories.

2. Prepare for the future.

It's understandable that if you're just getting started, that's your primary focus, but you also need to think about the future. Develop a succession plan that you review and revise annually.

3. Don't reinvent the wheel.

Look around for good ideas and good products that people are already using that you can incorporate into your operation. Everything you do doesn't have to be original; get ideas from other brokers, carriers, shippers and even totally unrelated businesses.

Bloomingdale, Illinois freight broker Ron Williamson learned this the hard way when he hired someone to develop a proprietary computer system. "That was a mistake because it wasn't a totally integrated system that would save us time and make us more efficient," he recalls. "Later on, we found a packaged program that had all the bells and whistles we needed."

4. Get rid of carriers that don't perform.

Every trucking company will have an occasional service problem, but when the service failures become chronic, drop the carrier from your roster. "You won't keep your customers very long if you're having constant problems with your carriers," says Ron Williamson. Of course, he acknowledges that, in the beginning, you probably won't know who all the good and bad carriers are. While it's one thing to be understanding and give a carrier a second chance, you need to draw the line before the problems affect your own business.

5. Maintain a broad and diverse customer base.

You need enough customers so that losing one—or even several—isn't devastating. One of the biggest mistakes Davis ever made when she ran her freight brokerage was allowing one customer to control too much of her company's revenue. When that customer pulled away with very little notice, she was left scrambling to replace that business.

6. Get in the Spotlight.

Because the freight industry is such a strongly relationship-and reputation-based business, it helps to put yourself in the public eye in a positive way as often as you can. Davis saw a favorable impact on her business from being the recipient of awards and by getting bylined articles published in trade publications.

7. Be open to evolution.

Though a freight brokerage is extremely lucrative on its own, it's also a business that can lead to the development of other transportation-related operations, from consulting to buying trucks and being a carrier. Cherry Hill, New Jersey freight broker Bill Tucker, for example, offers a wide range of logistics services.

8. Protect your reputation.

"Focus on building the highest-quality reputation you possibly can," advises Tucker. "When a shortcut presents itself but it's a little on the shady side, have the fortitude to pass it by, no matter how big the opportunity may seem. There are so many people in this industry who need good, solid, honest, reputable service, and long term, that's where the big money is. You survive, and you won't have a lot of doors closing because some bad story got out."

Tucker compares the industry to a small village. "Everybody knows everybody else's business. It's amazing how fast word travels. Nothing will put you out of business or limit your success faster than the story of one bad transaction or one nasty court loss because of bad practices getting out into the marketplace. You're going to have to sweat for a while, pull your belt in once in a while, and [endure] some tough times. But do it the right way every time, don't take any shortcuts, provide high-quality service and maintain your integrity, and you'll always have customers willing to pay a fair price and good carriers that want to work with you."

CHAPTER FIVE

HOW TO COLD CALL

Cold-calling a client is often regarded as the equivalent of clutching at straws regarding generating business—and research has shown that out of all prospecting methods, cold-calling is the least effective. The perceived wisdom against cold-calling states that its effectiveness disappeared when society moved into the Information Age and many sales gurus will state that cold-calling has not only become obsolete, inefficient and ineffective, it is actually counter-productive.

For sure, cold-calling is not for every sales team or every product or service, but for certain services, cold-calling is very useful in finding prospects willing and able to purchase and is an extremely effective prospecting tool. Because cold-calling, making an unsolicited business approach, either by doorstepping or by phoning, like spamming, is surprisingly successful if done well and, above all, is targeted and qualified.

The general principles of selling apply equally to cold-calling and is a normal sales call which is all about building a business relationship around a mutually defined need. A financial salesman once told me that when he called ten clients and closed a deal on the last one for one thousand dollar, each one of those calls wasn't actually worth nothing to him. That's the way he looked at it. Rather than nine rejections, each call was regarded as a success and precursor to the successful last one on which the deal was made.

The following are my top tips for being successful in your prospecting:

➤ **Homework:**

✓ Firstly, identify your market for your product or services. Next, target buyers in that market. Narrow the search and get an updated list of potential clients along with contact phone numbers etc. Be aware that your current clients competitors are a good starting point for new engagements.

✓ Invest time in research about your potential clients. The sales team need to be encouraged to research companies they are going to 'cold-call,' so they know something about the company's business, issues and as a result of their potential needs.

➤ **Doing the Call:**

The objectives of the call is to get the 30 minute appointment or a 'call to action'; a follow-up.

- ✓ Warm up the cold call by sending out a message that you will be calling (but do not say when). A cold call is better used for when you want to make a sale or make an appointment today – 'I am in your area today so.'

- ✓ Craft a good script and more or less stick to it—set down your exit dialogue and leave the door open preferably with a 'call-to-action.' However, customise the delivery and be contingent - the prospect may cut in and go directly to 'so what can you do for me...?'

- ✓ When starting the call, get to the point and be efficient. Never ask how they are today—it sets off invisible alarm bells and gives them time to think of a response to get you off the phone quicker than you expect.

- ✓ Smile and be pleasant throughout and you will feel better (and have higher self-esteem) and your client will feel that you are smiling through the reflection in your voice.

- ✓ Be nice to the gatekeepers and develop standard scripts to the objections they will throw at you. If you meet a new one (objection, that is) that you have not heard before, write it down and develop a scripted response for the next time it comes up.

✓ When you get to the principal, acknowledge a time limit and stick to it. 'I know you might have only 30 seconds so ...' Ask for the appointment and ask them to write it down.

✓ Get lot's of practice and develop yourself—I am quite serious—practice cold-calling on your colleagues and get them to give you a hard time (they will need little encouragement). They will be over the top but, nevertheless, this will be invaluable training.

Prospecting is the foundation of any company's sales approach and enables you to hit targets and fill the pipeline—it is the lifeblood of your sales process. What prevents people from cold-calling is often the fear of rejection that may abruptly occur. We need to turn this around—just as when fishing, we rue the nine that got away. But all that is forgotten when we land the big one. Besides, what has happened is that the client has not rejected you, she has lost the chance of a great deal for the short term ego-boost that chewing out a sales rep has given her.

Although each call will roll out differently, here are the main points you want to cover during the call:

1. **Opening introduction:**

Briefly introduce yourself with enthusiasm i.e., "Hi, this is John Smith." Don't bother asking an open-ended question like "How are you" or "Is this a good time to talk" because it just gives the person a chance to get you off the phone.

2. **Give a brief explanation of your work background and your level of experience.**

That is, "I'm a Database Administrator with five years of hands-on experience and I'm contacting you to enquire about your requirements for someone with my skillset." Then follow up with something exceptional and specific that makes you stand out from other candidates ie. "I am certified on Database Platform A and B and in my most recent position, I reduced database downtime by 23%." I think it's good to pop in a quick reference to the fact that you're a job searcher, without specifically asking for a job. At this point, all you are trying to do is get in front of them for an interview. That's the goal of the call. You don't want to put the person off by coming right out and asking for a job, but at the end of the day, that's your ultimate goal. No sense in beating around the bush and making it seem like you're calling them to have a chat. You made the call for a purpose and that purpose is to let them know why they need to do business with you.

3. **Ask for an interview. i.e. "When can you meet in person?"**

Again, these three points may only form part of the cold call because it will depend on what the person on the other end of the phone respond with. These three points are the main ones you want to get across during the call.

Potentially, cold-calling is a means of identifying potential prospects for your sales efforts. And is the main thing before any battle begins and is an excellent method of qualifying potential leads. Cold-calling is not where the sale happens its where the terrain is identified and the process begins. It must be said that cold-calling is hard work and not particularly effective compared to other techniques such as networking although, the most universally despised aspect of the sales job if done well will pay very rich dividends.

CHAPTER SIX

COLD CALL SCRIPT

There are cold-calling scripts available for free or for a fee. You can read those scripts word for word or absorb the words and speak from memory. Yet the results you want seem to be just out of reach.

Why is that happening? What is wrong with the scripts? Are the writers holding something back? Better yet, what do you need to do to get a script to work for you and get you where you want to go?

Firstly: words are important, but there is more to the cold-calling script picture than words. The order of your words is critical. They get you from "Hello" to the end of the call. The words are the roadmap to the call. Although the call will last a maximum of 90 seconds, you do need a plan; an effective script is such a plan. The words you choose to use are equally important. They tell your prospect whether or not you know the lingo of decision makers.

If you can talk-the-talk, your prospects think, maybe you can provide a much-needed business solution. Conversely, if you cannot talk-the-talk, you will never get past the Gatekeeper.

Still, in order to get predictable, successful outcomes with your cold-calling scripts you need much more than words. You must understand the unspoken communication as well as the words that are said. The way you speak, the underlying emotions behind the script will be recognized by your prospect immediately. Even when you do not want them to know how you are feeling, your prospects will know. They will know if you are a player who belongs in the decision-makers' circle or someone who really belongs with the low-levels of the organization. They will know whether or not you are fearful. They will know whether or not you are confident. In the face of this realization, a sales professional has to ask, do I know as much about myself as my prospects know from one cold call? Probably not.

To reap the rewards of cold calling, there is a learning curve and a price to pay. The cost is for you to get out of your comfort zone; successful callers do what it takes to replace fearful thoughts with empowering thoughts. They cultivate high-level verbiage and thinking. Decide to make these changes and you will find a stunning change in your confidence that will radiate throughout each prospecting call. Your tone alone will convey that you have what your prospects need; that is the real power of successful cold call scripts.

Here is a quick and easy way to pinpoint where exactly you are in the process. Call a colleague or family member. Leave a voice mail message of your cold call script. Ask the listener to give it to you straight. Ask, "Based on that script would you do business with me?" If the answer is yes, then hit the phones and get appointments. If they waffle or answer, no, then work the process through until you can say with confidence, absolutely I know they will do business with me.

DOES COLD CALLING SCRIPTS REALLY WORK?

This is the question that runs through the mind of so many people, but here is the answer to your curiosity; cold calling scripts seem to be in high demand, and thousands of salespeople are looking for the "magic bullet" cold calling script that they can rattle off over the phone, and start racking up sales.

So, that begs the question: Do cold calling scripts work?

❖ **My Experience with Cold Calling Scripts**

My first few years in sales were ugly; I was a miserable failure at getting leads and appointments, which led to a lot of job-hopping on my part until I finally figured out the sales game.

On that note, I began reading books about cold calling scripts. I was taught in my initial job training that I should stick to a script, which I'd get really good at and therefore add consistency to my cold calling results.

❖ **Others' Experience with Cold Calling Scripts**

The feedback I've gotten on cold calling scripts in training and working with thousands of salespersons' over the past several years, has been almost the same:

I say "generally" because there are people out there using the so-called "Cold Calling 2.0 scripts where you convince people and make your way in, which of course promote the sales at the end when you meet with the prospect, they realize you have worked through professional ways to get to them coupled with your experience.

In this case, the scripts "work" as far as getting you an appointment and those who make it this far—they WIN!

❖ **What About Sales Appointment Scripts?**

What about the idea of following a script in a sales appointment? Or on the phone, if your sales cycle is such that you work entirely on the phone without meeting prospects in person? (The latter was the case with my first 'real' sales job, selling business credit reporting services to business owners over the phone).

Sales scripts seem like a good idea on the surface. After all, at the point you'd start using them, you're already in an appointment with a prospect who has been identified as a lead. What's wrong with following a script at this point?

There's plenty wrong with it;

❖ Scripts Make You Seem Phony

The problem with following a scripted appointment is that you come across as phony. You're not being genuine, and thanks to the 93% of our communication that is non-verbal. The prospect knows this, no matter how good your script may be.

❖ People Buy People

It's true that your price, your reputation, the value of your offering, and many other factors come into play when a prospect chooses to buy. But they are not the biggest factors.

For instance, it's a known fact that among the top life insurance companies, prices are about the same and the companies are equally solid and financially sound. Despite this, only a handful hold the overwhelming majority of the market share.

Why?

People! Most life insurance policy owners have no idea what's in their policies, and even more astounding, they don't seem to care. The real reason they bought is because of the genuineness and pleasing personality of the salesperson they bought from.

And you know what a script does to a personality?

❖ **IT KILLS IT!**

You can't have a genuinely pleasing personality if your sales presentation is scripted and is not actually coming from YOU!

Politicians know this. Here in Texas we know our governor, Rick Perry, as a loud, back-slapping type of guy with a very magnetic personality. We were astounded to see his poor performance in the presidential debates.

And the reason for his poor performance is simple: for the first time in his life, he's operating from a script and from pre-rehearsed sound bites, instead of BEING HIMSELF like he always had in the past.

So if you want to be a really successful salesperson, one of the very top of the top performers, throw away the scripts - no, better yet, BURN THEM - and learn how to convey your own personality in a genuine way while also controlling the sales process to the desired point.

1. Build control into your cold call scripts.

As you script your call, then, make a statement; follow that statement with a question. Repeat that pattern throughout each call. Capture your prospect's attention with an informational driven statement. Then, engage them in the conversation with a question. Guide the course of the call with your questions. Make sure that your question leads toward the goal of scheduling an appointment. For instance: I am calling for a 20-minute meeting (statement). Do you handle his calendar or does he (question)?

2. Make sure your cold call scripts position you as the expert.

During each call, address the unspoken question upfront before your prospect asks, that question is - what is in it for your prospect if your prospect makes time to talk to you?

3. End each call with one of three pieces of information:

A meeting with the prospect; if necessary.

An agreement on the time to call back to schedule that meeting.

A good reason that the prospect is not the one with whom you will do business. This happens rarely. A viable reason could be that the company is going out of business.

Finally, the vital component is to make your one, single-minded goal to schedule an appointment. It doesn't matter if you want to arrange a face-to-face meeting or formal phone meeting; the process is the same.

WHAT SHOULD YOUR COLD CALLING SCRIPT INCLUDE?

Is your cold-calling script a source of grief and aggravation? If yes, do not worry. You are not alone; every single cold-calling script needs a thorough examination.

I know you do not need one more thing on your to-do list. However, this particular task will pay you back in new sales-revenues generated. That kind of payback is well worth the time invested. The next thing are the few opening lines of a newbie's cold-calling script.

The cold caller asked, "why are my calls forwarded to voice mail before the administrative assistant (AA) knows what I am calling about?"

Well, if you want to become perpetually stuck in voice mail jail, then, be sure to use the same words this caller used. Here it is, the script that faithfully fails to get the appointment and succeeds in getting a transfer to voice mail:

Caller: Mark Johnson, please.

AA: May I ask who is calling?

Caller: Sure this is - your Name - calling from - Name of Your Company.

AA: Just a Moment.

The administrative assistant sends the call to voice mail. The caller leaves a voice mail message, something to the effect of this; I am calling about marketing. Please, call me back.

The autopsy: The caller fails to state the purpose of the call. Without a purpose or compelling reason to listen to the caller, the administrative assistant simply directs the call to voice mail. True, the caller has just spoken a few opening lines. However, a lot more could have been said in those few sentences.

From the caller's perspective, being directly transferred to voice mail without further conversation is beyond rude. From the administrative assistant's perspective, an immediate transfer to voice mail is kind, avoids a thanks-but-no-thanks confrontation that would have predictably occurred had there been more conversation, and is the best way for the assistant to get rid of a caller who clearly does not know what he/she is doing. The assistant is thinking: if the caller is clueless during the prospecting call, how badly will they behave with the boss?

To breathe life into your cold call script: As you state your name, also state the purpose of your call and reason for the administrative assistant to connect you to a live person. Such as I am calling for a 20-minute meeting (purpose) to determine whether or not we can double the results of your marketing efforts (reason).

Autopsy, your own cold calling script, tweak it with tips you pick up, and expect an increase in sales revenues and commissions as a result of your efforts.

Preparing an effective cold call script

This will ensure that you get to communicate all that you need to within the shortest amount of time.

✓ **Personalize Each Call**

Using a script does not mean that you do not have the freedom to package each call as you find appropriate for each prospect. Your chances of success increase when your calls are personalized based on your objective. However, a script includes all the basic information that you require and that will propel them to make the decision to work with you or your company.

✓ Time limit

A cold call script also allows you to limit the amount of time that you take on the phone to meet a goal. To ensure that your script is effective, it is important to read aloud while timing yourself to determine the amount of time that it would take to make the cold call. For instance, it is important to politely identify yourself as well as your firm within the first 5 seconds, and then give the prospect a good reason to speak with you within the first 20 seconds.

✓ Engage The Prospect

The script should also have an allowance during which you ask the prospect about the possible problems that he or she could be facing. People would much rather talk about themselves than they would like to hear you talk about yourself. This is an important strategy in making a cold call more effective. You can achieve this by asking them a question that requires them to share their problems before you offer the solution.

✓ Deal with Obstacles

The script should also make room for objections and other obstacles that the prospect may present. Dealing with rejection should definitely be expected in any sales career, but it is also important to make your script as foolproof as possible. For instance, if a prospect says that he or she is very busy and will not be able to engage with you, ask if you could send an email so that the person could reply back when he or she has the time. You could even ask if the person would mind if you called again at a time of his or her choice. About 80 percent of new sales are made after the fifth contact, so persistence is critical in effective cold calling.

CHAPTER SEVEN

HOW TO NEGOTIATE RATES

Freight negotiations don't need to be like poker games, where only one side can win the pot.

Negotiation is something logistics professionals will be called upon to conduct many times throughout their careers. It comes with the territory. Successful negotiation is essential in business—especially when the economy is struggling. Everyone strives for the best value and the lowest costs when obtaining the best service possible.

Unfortunately, however, when it comes to freight negotiations, many companies specialize in the "win-lose" approach; a positional or distributive negotiation whereby one party's gain is another party's loss.

In win-lose bargaining, both parties are in direct competition and there can be only one winner.

Understandably, many people look at win-lose as a kind of game. Indeed, it can be compared to poker in that it is adversarial in nature, with both sides trying to win the pot through keen observance of an opponent's weaknesses, and a strategic use of bargaining chips. The big difference, of course, is that win-lose negotiations are not a game. And the stakes are very real.

Poker players like to play their cards "close to the vest," careful not to share information or reveal too much to their opponent. The same is true in win-lose negotiations, where there is minimal disclosures to the other party. Furthermore, buyers avoid giving any clues (or "tells") that would reveal their true position. Good negotiators are known for their poker faces. They 'hold' and 'raise' as necessary with pressure tactics and they pressure their opponents through delays, walkouts, and threats.

How effective is this approach to negotiations? Not very. It is often counterproductive and does not have any long-term sustainability.

Even when you win in this confrontational style of business, you still lose because the relationship with your counterpart is irreparably damaged. If you win enough your opponent will eventually stop playing the game. No one likes to lose, and they certainly don't appreciate being bullied. As the relationship deteriorates, the winner can expect the tables to turn when their opponent gets even by providing substandard service and at a lower cost in an effort to recoup losses.

In win-lose negotiations, logistic professionals are taking a short-term view, potentially locking their companies into a narrow range of positive outcomes. Win-lose does not serve the long-term interests of the winner, even if short-term objectives are achieved.

"Win-win" negotiations, on the other hand, involve integrative bargaining or interest-based bargaining, where the parties collaborate to find a mutually beneficial solution.

In the win-win approach to freight negotiations, both the shipper and carrier are engaged in finding the best solutions to move freight economically. It yields a freight agreement that each party is willing to fulfill.

Successful logistics buyers looking to achieve the best outcomes use win-win techniques where both parties in the negotiation walk away with the sense they have accomplished their objectives. Relationships are developed that have a foundation of trust because they are mutually beneficial. At the heart of the negotiation is true cooperative problem solving, cost cutting, customer service, and mutual profit.

This kind of collaboration takes additional work on the part of the logistics buyer. Here are six tips to help you negotiate rates in a way that has the greatest impact on your bottom line:

1. Preparation

This is the most important element in achieving an agreement... and it starts long before you sit down at the table. It involves a lot of data gathering.

First, understand the shipment. What is the size? The weight? The average cube per shipment? What kind of commodity is it? Is it dangerous? Does it have special requirements? Will it need temperature controls? Additional security? Dunnage?

Next, you have to know your customer's requirements. How much will be shipped? How often? What are the delivery locations? What about the dockside requirements? Unloading equipment at consignee? Dock? Tailgate? Pallet?

Now, what kind of equipment will be required? Dry van? Reefer? Heated service? Flat bed? Tridem? Tandem?

And finally, what is the service cycle time? What is the best mode of transportation?

Proper preparation will help you understand the implicit costs. Use benchmarking, historical data, industry associations, and the Internet to map out what you need. Based on this information, the shipper can set flexible objectives. They'll consider what would be the ideal situation, the very best that can be achieved. They'll also get a sense of the biggest challenges they'll face.

Preparation also involves finding the right transportation suppliers to negotiate with. Research and qualify the carriers that can provide the services you require. Find out as much about the companies as you can, the lanes they service, their service objectives, their response to damages, their reputation in the market place, the corporate culture they have fostered... anything that will help with the discussion.

2. Exchanging Information

At preliminary meetings with potential partners, a frank and open discussion is the best way to meet objectives. Shipment data is shared and service requirements are discussed. Where the sides differ, their expertise will be needed to improve the cost and service.

3. Making a Deal

When you're close to an agreement, have the carrier provide the full cost and service proposal electronically in advance of the meeting. This allows you to prepare for the meeting. Analyze the quote against current shipping data to understand the value proposition. The meeting agenda should consist of a discussion to understand services, rates, fuel surcharges and accessorial charges, as well as process improvements.

There is no room now for misconceptions. Don't be afraid to ask the carrier representative how rates can be lowered. Talk about what needs to be done. Never assume the amount quoted is the final price—most carriers' rates have some "wiggle" room.

The steps you take to improve the transportation deal are important blocks to building a solid relationship. Some concessions may have to be provided, to get lower costs, but it is worth it. Problem solving must be done jointly.

Focus on the issues at hand; don't take positions, and be flexible, using fair business practices. Most important, use reason not control, pressure, or power. Listen to what is being said. Find ways to make your freight attractive to the carrier.

This is true win-win negotiating, and it ensures that in the long run, everyone wins.

4. Study your shipping stats.

Think about the information that you provide FedEx and UPS— everything from customer names and addresses to the value of your products and other accounting information—and all the information they can gather about you because you're a customer, such as how much you spend on certain services and the average weight of your packages. They know a whole lot about your business, which gives them an advantage when you negotiate with their pricing team. Make sure you know everything they're going to be able to find out by scrutinizing your invoices. You don't want to go into this process with just a rough idea of your shipping preferences and spending with a carrier.

5. Know your top surcharges.

Get a good understanding of which surcharges have the biggest impact on your shipping operations so you can work to negotiate discounts on these charges. It's important to realize that some surcharges (like the more common fuel and residential delivery surcharges) will be harder to get discounts on than others, but it doesn't hurt to try.

6. Don't be distracted by value-add services.

Carriers typically use "value-add services" as one of their compelling arguments against further discounting your rates and will try to use these as a way to draw focus away from shipping fees, common surcharges and other key pricing factors. Be clear with your carriers that you appreciate these value-add services but that they're not going to impress you as much as competitive discounts and incentives.

7. Keep your contracts to yourself.

Keep your contracts to yourself! Providing one carrier a proposal from another carrier doesn't help you—you're basically giving them the tools they need to offer you just a slightly better deal. Keep this information to yourself to be used as leverage.

8. Stand your ground with refunds and penalties.

Late deliveries result in unhappy customers and lost opportunities for repeat business, which is why you should never waive your right to file for a money-back service guarantee or guaranteed service refund. You're paying for a specific service standard and will lose the ability to reclaim substantial money in the form of refunds if the carriers do not meet that standard.

You should also reject any contract language regarding early termination. Carriers raise your rates each year, and you shouldn't have to pay them a fee if you want to move your business elsewhere for cheaper rates. The only time you might consider accepting early termination language is if the carrier promises to freeze your rates for the term of the contract.

9. Diversify your shipping mix.

Don't put all your eggs in one basket—always keep a small amount of business with the other carriers. Try to keep 30 percent of your deliveries with another carrier (such as USPS, consolidators and regional carriers), because you never know when a rate will change or a new surcharge will pop up that will make you want to move more shipping volume to a different carrier. Letting your carrier know you also ship through other providers can give you an advantage, as the carrier will want to do what's possible to bring more of your business over.

TOSH COLE

CHAPTER EIGHT

HOW TO DISPATCH

Dispatch is a procedure for assigning employees (workers) or vehicles to customers. Industries that dispatch include taxicabs, couriers, emergency services, as well as home and commercial services such as maid services, plumbing, HVAC, pest control and electricians.

With vehicle dispatching, clients are matched to vehicles according to the order in which clients called and the proximity of vehicles to each client's pick-up location. Telephone operators take calls from clients, then either enter the client's information into a computer or write it down and give it to a dispatcher. In some cases, calls may be assigned a priority by the call-taker. Priority calls may jump the queue of pending calls. In the first scenario, a central computer then communicates with the mobile data terminal located in each vehicle (see computer assisted dispatch). Whereas, in the second scenerio, the dispatcher communicates with the driver of each vehicle via a two-way radio.

With home or commercial service dispatching, customers usually schedule services in advance and the dispatching occurs the morning of the scheduled service. Depending on the type of service, workers are dispatched individually or in teams of two or more. Dispatchers have to coordinate worker availability, skill, travel time and availability of parts. The skills required of a dispatcher are greatly enhanced with the use of computer dispatching software.

Trucking dispatch

Trucking dispatchers play a major role in transportation logistics. Truck dispatchers orchestrate freight movement and equipment from one place to another while keeping close communication with truck drivers. Some dispatching companies help truck drivers to negotiate and acquire loads and handle paperwork. Dispatching trucks require a variety of skills like using a computer to find and track loads for drivers to speaking multiple languages depending on the region or number of trucks they manage. Great customer service and good communication skills are vital for succeeding in this fast-paced environment.

Freight Dispatch

Freight dispatchers are employed by trucking companies to coordinate shipping operations with drivers, suppliers and receiving customers. They may work with company drivers or may coordinate with other carriers to find available drivers to cover loads of freight. A freight dispatcher schedules truck arrivals for product pickup and delivery and tracks the progress of transit to ensure on-time deliveries. Dispatchers also work with trucking company customers to record freight orders and resolve billing issues. These job duties demand strong skills in written and oral communication, multi-tasking, organization and customer service.

Mostly, dispatchers work in an office environment, though they may be required to help load or unload freight as needed. As such, you generally need to be physically fit and able to lift up to 50lbs, and the work is often more physically demanding than that of other dispatchers in other industries.

JOB DESCRIPTION OF A DISPATCHER

> **Strong Communications Skills Needed**

Truck dispatchers need to have at least a high school diploma or equivalent, excellent communication skills and a strong command of the English language to ensure drivers understand their instructions. Successful truck dispatchers also need to have excellent time-management skills and the ability to work in high-pressure situations and fast-paced environments. Because one of their main duties is to prioritize drivers' schedules, superior organizational abilities are required.

➢ **Road Experience Not Needed**

Although some drivers become successful dispatchers, it is not necessary for a truck dispatcher to have driving experience. While on-the-road experience is helpful for supporting new drivers or gaining familiarity with Department of Transportation regulations, on-the-job training can be enough. Being comfortable working with computer software is important because many trucking companies keep track of their drivers' schedules with sophisticated computer applications. Because communication skills are so important, truck dispatchers benefit from having previous experience in a decision-making role. Experience with coordinating groups of people or tasks also helps.

➢ **Driving Home Duties and Responsibilities**

Truck dispatchers work in a centralized location coordinating and managing the delivery of ground-transported cargo. Days tend to be very busy and the workload constant. Truck dispatchers spend part of their days negotiating the best rates with vendors, the most cost-effective delivery options with customers and the most efficient routes with drivers, all while answering phones when drivers need assistance. They also fulfill an administrative role by filing the appropriate paperwork, monitoring driver progress, processing orders and managing driver concerns.

Qualities Of A Good Dispatcher Include:

- ✓ High moral character and integrity
- ✓ Compassion
- ✓ Good judgment
- ✓ High degree of emotional self control
- ✓ Empathy and sensitivity
- ✓ Intelligence
- ✓ Good communication skills
- ✓ Self confidence
- ✓ Creativity and ingenuity
- ✓ Strong desire to serve the company
- ✓ Effective at multi-tasking

Things Truck Dispatchers Should Do Every Day

1. **Have a software that helps them.**

It is very hard to follow the process only by a manual work, it requires a lot of time a lot of concentration a lot of energy and it can be very hard even for the best ones.

Having a program that can assist with this information is one step closer to a well done job:

- ✓ Keeping records of the truck driver daily steps for errors or violations
- ✓ Following truckers behavior and keeping him legal on the road
- ✓ Keeping track of the weather where the truck drivers are or headed to
- ✓ Determine the best delivery methods and negotiate rates
- ✓ Identify and evaluate any special needs for each load
- ✓ Advise the truck driver to avoid construction areas, accidents, traffic problems or other hazards
- ✓ Prioritize time sensitive cargo
- ✓ Keeping up with maintenance
- ✓ Automatic and accurate IFTA calculations
- ✓ Customer information
- ✓ Fast generation of invoices
- ✓ Recorded miles
- ✓ Automatically sorted fuel gallons by state
- ✓ Automatic generation of billing details
- ✓ Plan for delivering the most profitable routes
- ✓ Record information of who delivered what and to where
- ✓ Keeping the customers happy
- ✓ Keep your drivers safe

✓ Alerts the truck driver about traffic problems such as construction areas, accidents, congestion, weather conditions, and other hazards.

2. They will recommend the best route to the driver.

Improve the planning process and make sure your truck drivers are taking the shortest possible route. Reducing the number of miles for your truck drivers will help you to have more satisfied customers and will help your company to reduce fuel consumption. These steps for sure will help you to run your business more successfully.

3. They should be well informed about the economy.

Keeping track on the economy is the best way to prevent your company from unexpected costs:

- Fuel Cost Increases – if your cost for a shipment cannot cover fuel costs, driver wages, or the other undercurrent transportation costs, because you missed the information of the sudden increase of the fuel price, your company will suffer heavy losses.

- Demand for trucking – with increased economy expansion proportionally we have increased demands for overall dispatch.

Important task for every dispatcher is to catch on time updates for every economic change that may influence the trucking business.

4. They should know their drivers habits.

Truck drivers have negative and positive habits. Knowing that your truck driver:

- o Is a responsible driver;

- o Observes and obey the rules on the road;

- o And completes all necessary documents correctly and accurately

Gives you a sense of security. For this type of driver you need to make occasional checks, you need to give him daily updates and instruction and he will know what to do.

Keep track on the hours of service. Be sure he is doing everything right, do not give him a chance to put his life in danger or to bring the company to an inconvenient situation.

Make sure the truck is in perfect condition or react otherwise, regular maintenance gives secure loads.

Providing correct info can be helpful for the company to invest in driver training, to allow special attention on a specific situation or on the problematic behavior.

5. **They should have effective and personal connection with the brokers.**

Freight brokers are an individual or company, connection between the shipper and the carrier. With a good freight broker at your side you have less worries, that is why strong and personal connections with the brokers is a smart thing to do.

Connections they are having with the shippers are useful for every truck company, they fill the carrier trucks with loads and for that service they earn commission, more work brings more money.

6. **They should know all about their company trucks (location).**

When you know your truck location, you are able to give support and reliable information, in this way you will secure effective continuity in your company.

7. **They think one step in advance and start looking for connected loads.**

Having a clear and precise list of the current loads, will give you an advantage towards making effective load schedules; be aware of the loads that are nearby and inform the truck driver to pick up those loads, connect them and save time and money.

Imagine the additional cost the company will have if you missed this information. Sending another truck driver in the same location where some of your trucks have been before at the same time or short time after is unnecessary cost for the company. Find the best schedule method for shipments.

Improve your planning process, locate, prepare and assign the truck drivers for taking certain loads. This is the reason why a dispatcher must be highly organized and be able to handle high amounts of information.

8. They should always be available to their drivers.

Keep in touch and be available, give them updates and require the same in return. With the information received in the right moment you can prepare more loads.

Prioritize to be available to your drivers, in this way you can step up and make intervention if that is necessary. Solving the obstacles in the right way at the right place can protect your company from missed opportunity or load delays.

9. Pay attention to details.

We are all individuals with different characteristics some are naturally born with this feature others have to learn how to develop over the time. Best prevention of mistakes is paying attention to details.

FREIGHT BROKER WITH CARE

Overlooking details can be dangerous it can cost your company amounts of money or clients. Learn how to make a connection of everything and with everything, take a look at the big picture.

10. Check the following few tips, they may help you.

Schedule: Make a schedule, prepare yourself for the day.

Make a list. Put all of your tasks in one place, this will help you to stay updated after interruptions, you will not forget what you should do after. Cross the task after you are finished, this feeling will give you motive to go to the next task and to keep going until you complete all of your tasks.

Check for accuracy and consistency. Always check your work or documents before you take them to the next step, better spend a bit more time instead of sending false information to the collegues; that will create a chain reaction that can cost a lot.

Create a detailed work plan. Help yourself to focus and learn to take the most important task at the moment.

Learn to multitask. Dispatchers are the moving force in the company a lot of people depend on your efficiency and speed, learn to multitask to keep everybody around in order at the same time.

Develop great problem-solving skills. Be able to prioritize the most important situations at the moment and think quickly.

Limit distraction. Make sure your environment is distraction free and use your time efficiently to complete the assignments.

Do not overload yourself. Pressure can cause panic and a blockage in your brain, keep you tasks realistic.

Frequent walks. These will re-energize your body.

- ✓ Always be prepared for negotiations about the load price.

- ✓ Dispatchers have to be calm to be in control of the situation especially in emergency circumstances.

- ✓ Excellent communication skills gives you advantage over the situation.

- ✓ Your ability to speak, listen and analyze the conversation gives you power to affect on the process to lead to a successful outcome.

- ✓ It is always good to be polite especially when you are a dispatcher. Sometimes you may run into a nervous client, remember your voice is your power tool to keep the situation under control. Excellent communication skills open doors to new possibilities.

STEPS ON HOW TO DISPATCH FREIGHT SUCCESSFULLY

In order to successfully dispatch a truck once you accept a load from your customer, be sure to retrieve the following:

o Pick up location (Address); contact name; and phone number.
o Consignee (Address) same
o Any special pickup or delivery requirements

Get this information now so that you can go back and negotiate these additional requirements to the carrier upfront, add in your percentage and get approval for those additional charges so that you will not jeopardize having to bite the fee's at the end.

❖ Always call to let them know when you expect your truck arriving; ask the shipper if your driver need some sort of pick up number to get on dock; by asking all necessary questions alleviates any unexpected surprises.

❖ Now that you have all the accurate information needed for the truck to arrive and deliver successfully, now it's time to get the driver on the line and dispatch for a successful trip.

❖ Get driver info such as name, truck number, trailer number, direct contact number and make sure your driver is empty and fueled up.

Get Current Location and "Go Time"

1. Google the driver current location and the address to the pickup location to ensure that the driver have the best route in mind; by doing this you can also alert the driver for any unforseen issues along their route.

2. Do an overview of the route then provide the driver with the shipper pickup location and appointment time scheduled; advise the driver whether or not the shipper location have any special requirements up front.

3. Tell the driver to make sure that once the shipper loads the freight that the seal is intact prior to leaving the location; this will prevent carrier liability for loss and damages during transit.

4. Update your system with a scanned copy of the bill of lading, the driver arrival and loading time and seal number, make sure that detention charges were not accrued because if so, most carriers charge around 60 bucks for each hour over their allotted time which is equivalent to $15.00 per increments of 15 minutes of each hour deemed late.

NOTE: If by chance the driver is late from loading and the expected delivery times are now altered, be sure to call the consignee and reschedule the delivery appointment. Most companies honor their delivery appointment times, even a couple of minutes off schedule can cause some unforeseen problems. Layover cost can accrue if the driver has to hold the freight on the trailer until another appointment date is arranged.

Now that the driver is loaded successfully:

- ➤ Follow the same procedures from when you dispatched the driver to the pickup location; make sure that you have accurate information, do an route comparison with the driver and advise of any special requirements, appointment date and times, specific dock numbers, appointment numbers etc.

- ➤ Find out when the driver will go on break, hours of rest and location. Depending on how far of a travel your driver has, they must understand that you are their contact person and if any issues arise during transit then you have to be called immediately.

- ➤ Request a courtesy check call twice a day; use your own judgment but if the driver has a 3day trip then you will like to provide some sort of update to your customer so as to make sure that you always know where the freight is at all times.

- ➤ Calculate the mileage of the driver's current location to the final destination and take in consideration the driver rest hours and fuel stops.

- ➤ Aim to provide the most accurate estimated arrival time when giving your status updates to your customer and Range every 50 miles equivalent to an hour of travel time for your driver during transit.

Now that your driver is all set and ready to go:

- Give your customer a courtesy call letting them know that the shipment is picked up and is on schedule for "on time" delivery. Assure your customer that you are on top of their shipment and that you will be tracking it around the clock and will advise if there are any issues along the way.
- The quickest way to get paid for your shipment is to make sure that your driver calls you when the shipment is empty. Make sure that you are provided a signed BOL copy which is commonly known as POD (proof of delivery).
- By providing your customer the signed POD copy, this completes the shipment and is typically the only thing needed so that you can get paid.

Once you conclude this shipment with your customer, this is the perfect time to ask about extra available loads and projects!

Also, take the time to reach back out to the shipper and consignee once your driver completes the full shipment; make sure that they had a nice experience with your driver; then ask if they need any assistance with any future shipments; find out if they are working on any projects, and that you can start putting together a strategy plan for them.

Remember, every opportunity counts towards higher load volumes and profit gain so please make sure that you utilize all resources effectively; you'll surely be well on your way towards becoming a successful freight broker.

CHAPTER NINE

HOW TO HANDLE CLAIMS AS A FREIGHT BROKER

I t's with some frequency that we come across freight claims that have been denied due to "Shipper Load & Count." The mere fact is that freight with "shipper load and count" is not reason enough to accept a declination of your cargo claim. In many cases, the claimant is in fact, due for reimbursement. This of course depend on many factors and most require research as well as changes to those internal policies and procedures that pertain to shipment discrepancies and how transportation claims are handled.

Having spent the better part of our careers as a freight broker serving the major retail and wholesale markets, we were able to develop and successfully implement a number of process changes and tracked the performance over time. These solutions have since made it possible for other brokers to significantly reduce recurring and declined SL&C freight claims.

Freight Claim Management

Firstly, it is strongly suggested that shippers use transportation contracts rather than the carrier's tariff. That is well crafted transportation contracts which mean enlisting the services of a transportation attorney. The contract should clearly define the procedures to which both parties will adhere as it relates to identifying and reporting overages, shortages and damage issues ("OS&D") to include the amount of time allowed. This will ensure reports are made at the soonest possible point after discovery. It is imperative that the contract should be free of references to the carrier's tariff since the tariff can change without notice and discrepancies between the two documents often results in future misunderstandings.

Secondly, incorporate key elements of the carriers' brokers Load and Count Agreement into your transportation agreement and insure all shipping personnel refrain from signing any documents presented by the carrier. Implementing an SL&C clause can be accomplished by adding only the language that is necessary as a rule in the Contract's "Rules Schedule."

Freight Claim Disputes

This talk about language has to do with any conflict between a bill of lading and the contract governed by the terms of the carrier contract. This is crucial to insuring consistency in how freight claims and disputes are handled. Many legal experts also recommend that brokers use their own version of the bill of lading where a number of clauses have been modified.

Another suggested change is the addition of a rule requiring carriers to provide written notification of any discrepancy found on a broker load and count trailer, and to provide this notification within a specified time frame. Included as an exhibit to the contract should be the standardized templates that the parties will use to report discrepancies. Processing instructions included on the template will further support compliance and the information ultimately provides a much clearer picture of exactly where freight loss or damage is occurring.

How to Write a Freight Claim

<u>What is a freight claim?</u>

There are alternative words, such as shipping/cargo/ transportation claim or loss and damage claim, and one would file such a claim to recover their costs from a carrier (not including profits), although in some cases claiming profits may be considered acceptable as well.

What details to include in your claim?

You need to bear in mind that most carriers (such as UPS or FedEx) provide their own forms for filing freight claims and you can usually download them from their websites. BUT, no particular form is necessary by law, as long as the following details are specified:

- The shipment;
- The loss or damage type;
- The total of the amount claimed;
- A clear demand for payment.

<u>The following documents should be provided:</u>

- Shipment invoice;
- Delivery receipt;
- Bill of lading;
- Invoice showing the value of the product being claimed;
- Invoices for costs incurred;
- Photos, police report, along with additional supporting documents as needed.

Also, It's useful to include some additional info, such as the vehicle number, order number and the carrier pro number, to identify the shipment.

Remember that if your claim is filled out incorrectly or some of the documents are missing, the chances of getting back your money are very slim; every detail and every piece of paper matters and should be handled with great care, which is why it might be a very good idea to hire a team of professionals to help you go through this multifaceted process with ease.

Deadlines

Another important thing to consider: For instance, UPS freight acknowledges claims within 30 days and some other international carriers' may give you up to 90 days. However, it's always a good idea to file your claim as soon as you can, meaning you should begin to collect the paperwork for your claim the moment you notice a loss or a damage. The longer you wait, the more chances there are to lose track of your records. That's another reason to delegate the filing of your freight claim to a firm that specializes on freight audit, or at least to make sure that there are people on your team who carefully inspect all your packages as soon as they arrive, every time.

What happens next?

Then you wait. The carrier is obliged to respond and they do in the end, but this may take longer than expected: usually, 30 to 90 days or even more. That's why we recommend for you to be organized and to use some kind of procedure that works for you, in order to track your claims and make sure you get a adequate response from the carrier. Again, a trained consultant may help you to come up with an effective procedure that works best in your business environment.

CHAPTER TEN

A TYPICAL DAY AS A FREIGHT BROKER

Freight brokers act as intermediaries by arranging for the transportation of loads between shippers and motor carriers. The freight broker then receives a commission for his or her matchmaking skills. Freight brokers are also known as truck brokers, transportation brokers, property brokers and 3rd party intermediaries.

While the business concept in freight brokering is very simple, there are many details and procedures that need to be mastered. The broker needs to know what to do, when to do it, how to do it, why it's being done and with whom to do it. Since this is a service-oriented business, it only makes sense to learn the multitude of demands and requirements - especially in light of the fast-paced environment that only seems to increase more and more.

While actual "on the job" experience is the best teacher, it's difficult to find brokers willing to employ new agents. Formal training with qualified individuals who have actual brokering experience helps pull everything into perspective for the beginning broker. As a result of using a good mentor, the new broker not only gets ahold of the tools of the trade but also strikes out on a note of confidence.

Having said this, let's take a look at a typical day in the life of a freight broker.

After the freight broker has placed many phone calls to potential customers, he or she should have perhaps 20, 30, 40 or more shippers in their database. The initial information that each broker will collect will be general in nature: what type of cargo is the shipper shipping, where are the normal pick up and deliver points, what kind of truck is required and so on.

   a) With a base of customers on hand, the broker will want to start asking for the order by placing phone calls to shippers early in the morning—perhaps from 7:30 AM to 10:30 AM. This is when most shippers are putting the final touches on their needs. Basically, the broker is asking if the shipper is looking for any trucks on that particular day.

b) If the answer is "No", the broker goes on to the next and the next. At some point, the broker hits a "hot" one (or several) and that's when the action begins.

c) After the broker has "proved" him or herself, the shipper will actually initiate calls to the broker instead of the broker always calling the shipper. And the shipper may want to work more proactively by looking for trucks 3-5 days out instead of just on a day-by-day basis.

d) Once the shipper has a load for which he or she needs a truck, the next step is to take the order from the shipper. The shipper will go into detail on what is required. Any uncertainties that the broker has should be cleared up immediately. It's imperative that the broker communicates the correct information to each truck driver or dispatcher when they start calling in.

e) Then the broker will either work up an estimate of what rate is needed and they'll get back with the shipper; or the broker will simply ask the shipper what they want to pay. After some calculations the freight broker will come up with an amount that they will offer to the truck. The ideal starting point is to get at least a 10% profit margin on each load.

f) The next step is to post these loads on the internet load boards. There are numerous loading boards where loads are posted as well as searches for trucks that may be done.

g) After these loads have been posted, the broker will then go to his or her database of available trucks. The broker will then call each carrier to see if they have a truck available. In the meanwhile, the broker may be receiving incoming calls from individuals who are responding to the posts on the load boards.

h) At some point, the broker is looking for the driver or dispatcher who will say, "Yes, I want the load". Sometimes the broker will not find a truck. This is not like shooting fish in a barrel; however, with experience and by earning repeat business, the broker will "cover" more and more loads.

i) After the broker gets the "Yes" from the carrier, he or she then immediately calls the shipper to tell them that the load is being booked.

j) The broker will then fax their set up package to the carrier. While the carrier is processing the agreement and other papers, the broker will check out the carrier to make sure the carrier is properly authorized and insured. This is done either on the internet or telephone.

k) The last item sent to the carrier is the "confirmation". The carrier should immediately sign and date this document and fax it back to the broker.

l) Once the broker has this confirmation on hand, the broker will want to call the truck driver if the driver himself hasn't called the broker. The details of the load are then given to the driver along with any instructions. For example, the broker will ask the driver to call when they get loaded and when they get empty or if there is any problem. The broker will also ask the driver to call in at least every morning if it is a multi-day trip. These are important requirements that each broker should be ready to implement.

m) After the load is delivered and the carrier has reported back to the broker, the broker will want to call the shipper to let them know of the status.

n) Any problems that may arise upon delivery which may include missing pieces or damaged cargo should be dealt with between the shipper and carrier. Sometimes the broker will intervene; however, the broker is never liable for any damage or missing pieces unless the broker is negligent.

o) Lastly, with the load delivered safely and in a timely fashion, the broker is ready to do the process over and over again.

While this routine may seem casual and boring at times—this is hardly the truth. Most of the time the broker will experience smooth going. However, there will be some times when problems will arise—late deliveries, failure of the carrier to pick up a load, damaged cargo or missing pieces, long delays in picking up or delivering cargo—all of these need to be dealt with by the broker.

It is impossible to avoid problems, but it is possible to stay alert and ready to deal with problems proactively. If the broker works hard and works smart for the shipper, if the broker deals honestly with the truck and pays them on time—the broker is well on his or her way to a successful venture.

CHAPTER ELEVEN

TIPS TOWARDS BECOMING A SUCCESSFUL FREIGHT BROKER

The most important part of a freight broker or agent's business is his book of clients. A good list of customers is where a broker or agent access to find freight to move. Of course, one should always be working on developing his list and finding new customers, but a strong list of people who have already done business with you, can provide business indefinitely, as long as you keep them happy.

To develop a list of customers who need your services, you will want to try a variety of resources. Most of your customers will be manufacturers needing to get their products to various buyers including distributors, retailers, and other supply chain members. Think of resources you could use to find companies needing to ship large amounts of goods, and start from there.

❖ Start with a low-cost TMS

Sure, that fancy transportation management system the salesperson pitched looks nice, but do you need all its functionality now? Whether you are digital or voice, you will need a backend system for managing loads. If you are going down the traditional route - you should be ready to go out of the box with a little more than some small configuration. In fact, you can get started for less than $50 per month, if you are not concerned about advanced functionality. Often, a low-cost cloud-based system, while more limited, is sufficient to build the business. As the money starts to roll in, you can always upgrade to that Cadillac TMS you really want.

❖ How do you count the money?

An often-overlooked system is the accounting system. Make sure you choose a system that can meet your needs, from payroll to accounts payable and receivables. Like the TMS, the accounting system doesn't have to be top-of-the-line, but it needs to be more than Bob in accounting jotting down notes in a ledger. Quickbooks offers a cloud-based option that can get you started, and there are other options available as well.

❖ How will you sustain the company?

Sure, every transaction will bring in some revenue and if the load is priced for margin (the spread between what you sell the service to the shipper and what you pay the carrier) - you will make money on paper. Unfortunately, this won't turn into cash overnight. Carriers will want to be paid within 20-30 days and shippers will pay in 40-90 days. The faster you grow, the more capital you will consume. That is, unless you set up an accounts receivable financing relationship. While traditional banks offer these lines, they have little experience in freight. We recommend looking for a firm that is familiar with A/R financing in trucking and can fund your working capital. In an earlier article, FreightWaves highlighted two companies, BAM Worldwide and Triumph Business Capital, they handle thousands of freight financing transactions per day.

FreightWaves dove into this subject: New twists in invoice factoring.

❖ Get an MC number

Brokers who are registering for the first time must apply for broker authority with the FMCSA via the Unified Registration System and get assigned an MC number. This identifies carriers who transport regulated commodities for hire in interstate commerce. The longer you have this number, the less risky you will look to carriers, leading to more of the accepting freight from your site.

❖ Get proper insurance

This should go without saying, but having proper insurance is a must. A few years ago, DAT provided some basics that insurance should cover. These include property and general liability; auto liability and umbrella; workers' compensation; contingent cargo; and errors and omissions.

You are in the freight matching business, and central to that business is understanding rates. Unless you are a rate expert, you need some help in forecasting and tracking rates. DAT offers several subscription options for rates and is widely recognized as the leader in this area.

❖ **Develop relationships with trusted carriers**

Having relationships with carriers you can count on is critical. The worst thing that can happen to any dispatcher is if loads are posted and never claimed. Consider using an onboarding platform for carriers, such as DAT's On Boarding, and utilize tools like Carrier 411 for vetting and monitoring of carriers.

❖ **Find your niche**

You want to broker freight, that's great. What kind? Are you going to accept any freight? Creating a niche can be a good way to build trust. If you handle only dry van and refrigerated freight, shippers and carriers specializing in these areas will identify easily with your site. If you choose to accept all types of loads, make sure the various types of loads are segmented properly – either through sections or search. A flatbed hauler who has to pass through 1,000 dry van loads to find a single flatbed load won't be a user of your service for very long. Also make sure location is a searchable function.

❖ Provide value-added management services

Simply matching loads to trucks is one thing, but if you want to stand out, develop a strategy for capacity sourcing and become a trusted advisor to carriers and shippers. This can include total cost of ownership data and understanding that freight transportation management isn't just about price.

❖ Join an association

To be involved in any industry requires connections. The Transportation Intermediaries Association is a trade association designed for third-party logistics providers and has plenty of networking opportunities. It also provides educational content and best practices among a multitude of benefits.

❖ Remember that business is about people

Organizations are only as strong as the people that make up the organization. Transportation is a close-knit community and it won't take long for stories of mistreatment to make the rounds. To avoid this, remember that your employees – and the carriers and shippers you deal with – are people who want to be treated with respect. Recruit strong people, retain good employees and provide incentives for jobs well done. An employee incentive program can also drive appropriate behavior and keep employees engaged.

CONCLUSION

I t is important before you begin selling to understand the ins and outs of freight and the transportation industry. Do you know what kind of specific requirements your customers might have, and how to arrange for them? What weight limitations are there? Does a shipment need refrigeration? You may also want to try specializing in a specific region or industry. Becoming an expert in moving a particular type of freight might make you more desirable to companies in these industries, and help you focus your client search as you start out. You can always expand as business grows. You can even take classes for a freight broker license. That can help you find more freight in areas that require licensing.

A freight broker agent must be persuasive and persistent as it would considerably enhance their skill set and increase effectiveness. The agent must always ensure that he has linked the right carrier to the right shipper as it would help them both in understanding the other's terms and would avoid any liabilities that may cost him his commission. If he is effective, he will be made a resident agent by the client, which is a mark of success as the agent would now steadily receive orders and would take care of all transactions by the same client, which would ease the entire process.

In addition, and in summary to what have been discussed earlier for the Best practice tips for Load Tracking success:

Make use of the Notes section. The Notes section can be used to relay any important information to the driver. It's a free text box, so click in the box and type your message.

Use full physical street addresses. To ensure the automated arrival and departure calls are completed, enter in the full physical street address for both in the Origin section, as well as local pickup date and time.

Change tracking times manually. Note that by default, tracking will start 6 hours prior to a scheduled pickup time. This can be adjusted based on your needs.

Set your geofence radius. What is geofencing? Using the location of the phone, geofencing triggers a ping to let you know your truck's either leaving or arriving at the destination.

Request required docs. The driver will be notified that a document is required for a event. You have the option to request documents for a given check call, and indicate which document is needed. If you have any documents you want to send to the driver, such as a BOL or rate con, you can do so by clicking the blue Add File button at the bottom in the Uploaded Files section.

Need to make edits? After submitting your request, if you need to make any edits to this track request or send additional docs at a later time, you will have the option to edit on the Track Details section.

To recap: Load Tracking is convenient, protects your drivers, and ensures your shippers know exactly where those loads are.

You offer the heightened transparent experience and you get the deals. And when it comes to brokering, every deal count.

Now that you know all the necessary steps you must take to get your freight broker license, we recommend you take a look at our other freight broker guides and follow the details carefully which cover some of the most important information you'll need to know regarding training, cold calling, making claims, freight dispatcher duties and how to leverage load boards to grow your brokerage. Take a look at some of the topics covered in our e-book guides below:

- ✓ The importance of training for freight brokers
- ✓ Freight broker software programs
- ✓ Need to know accessorial codes
- ✓ How to earn big as a new freight broker
- ✓ How to cold call
- ✓ Cold call script
- ✓ How to negotiate rates
- ✓ How to dispatch
- ✓ How to handle claims as a freight broker

- ✓ How to write a freight claim
- ✓ A typical day as a freight broker

These e-book guides were created specifically with freight brokers in mind, and provide all of the crucial information you need to help ensure your brokerage thrives in this competitive profession.

Much of what you have to know on how to become a freight broker or start a new brokerage business is covered in our freight brokering training guide. If you are following each step as described, I am confident you will succeed. You will be sure to get the right industry certifications to help you along your career.

www.ingramcontent.com/pod-product-compliance
Lightning Source LLC
Chambersburg PA
CBHW022008170526
45157CB00003B/1189